Praise for Jaime Luis Huenún and *Fanon City Meu*

Fanon City is Peru, it's Brazil, it's Bolivia, it's Ecuador, it's Alabama, it's Cuba, it's Mexico, it's Aruba or Curaçao. It's where Cesar Vallejo is in jail; it's the home of Che Guevara's disembodied hands. It is, perhaps, the whole of the Americas, united by a shared infection, a shared violence, a shared history of colonial murder. Jaime Luis Huenún, a Mapuche poet from southern Chile and author of *Port Trakl*, here extends his canon of literary cities built in homage to writers and the wars that form them. And *Fanon City Meu*, translated powerfully by Thomas Rothe, makes a hemispheric argument by creating a poem from the continuum of violence that begins with the European slaughter of the Americas and extends into the neoliberalist slaughter of Chile and the cultural and environmental degradation it has wrought. *Fanon City Meu* is "a poem of rats," a poem where the entwined disaster of genocide and capitalism must be acknowledged, analyzed and resisted. "Beware of national anthems," writes Huenún, as we move through the border checkpoints of nations that break their own people. *Fanon City Meu*, then, is a poetics of protest against those who have been deluded by centuries of colonial madness, and for those who survive and fight.

—**Daniel Borzutzky**, author of *The Performance of Becoming Human* (National Book Award, 2016)

In some quarters, the term "globalization" may yet have beneficent connotations. But in this remarkably powerful and prophetic collection of poetry by award-winning Chilean poet Jaime Luis Huenún (b. 1967), global means the planetary dissemination of inequality and rage accumulated over the centuries and deposited in a single society of new masters and slaves, who speak a mixture of languages on the honed blade of these poems that cut like a machete. Make no mistake. Huenún is not a poet who minces his words in *Fanon City Meu*. With a certain resignation capable of assimilating prior defeats and not exempt from bitterness, he presents his denunciation of these conditions from within an historical past that is simultaneously a message and an exhortation from the future.

—**Steven F. White**, editor of *El consumo de lo que somos: muestra de poesía ecológica hispánica contemporánea*

Fanon City Meu, by Jaime Luis Huenún and translated by Thomas Rothe, is a compelling collection of poetry, which dares us to look beyond our own realities and see a world that for so many is fraught with instability and danger. The legacy of colonization is alive and well, and its ignorance and viciousness is reflected in many of the lines of these candidly raw vignettes. The ghosts of lost freedom fighters and heroes also make appearances here because after all, it is we poets who must keep them alive. Amid the stark landscape here there are also poems that make us smile because love and hope peek through, "…the broken window of darkness." A million thanks for this collection because not everything in life is pretty and all of it must be witnessed. Saludos!

— **Odilia Galván Rodríguez**, editor of P*oetry of Resistance—Voices for Social Justice*, and author of *The Nature of Things*

Jaime Huenún is an extraordinary Mapuche poet, an extraordinary Chilean poet, and an extraordinary global poet. This book expands the horizon of his poetry and Chilean poetry like never before, proving itself planetary. Peripheral struggles, embodied in the eponymous figure of Frantz Fanon, are the backdrop over which we observe the transformations capitalist powers have forced onto the pre-modern and non-capitalist world since the sixteenth century—seldom without violence—and the contemporary and necessary responses. Blacks, zambos, mulattos, Altiplano and Mesoamerican Indians converted into laborers; Mapuches converted into laborers. The consequential emptying of ancestral memory, erased by the sweat of denigrating jobs, is one more consequence of that raid. "Life was not lost, pastoral brothers," Neruda nonetheless wrote in the first poem of his Canto General. What remains in the 21st century of those humiliated "pastoral brothers" are the poems contained in *Fanon City Meu*. Not the epic actions of old revolutionaries, those who grew old, died, and were eternalized in the marble statues of history's official narratives; rather the other, anonymous actions that now resurface in the form of an ancient and new brotherhood, reunited after centuries of living in the shadows. This is poetry that listens, that restores verse with the power of human sound, everyday speech. Poetry that communicates what it hears and also offends when necessary. Robust and honest poetry like none other I have read in today's flaccid Chilean Parnassus.

— **Grínor Rojo,** author of *Chile, Dictatorship and the Struggle for Democracy*

Fanon City Meu exists in the realm of translation. Jaime Luis Huenún's prose poems mold the cobble, dirt, and fibers of/ towards the making of decolonial subjects. Or rather, Huenún materializes the path towards decolonization, the illustrious and terrible, the remnants and gathering, the humorful and less so. Huenún reaches forwards (or is it back) to Chile, indigeneity, and the post-colonial subject with this collection, navigating the limits and uneven truths of locality, gender, and colonial departure. Here, we are reminded of the fodder and fuel Fanon himself offered, that indeed the structuring of the post was/is a type of incessant and poetic becoming.

— **Essence Harden,** UC Berkeley

To contemplate the "dreadful radiance of our History" should be uncomfortable for any conscious reader. Huenún's meditations put us all on the spot in a blurry mirror, warped by the heat of light. The mirror sags toward the bottom line, the surface of the Earth, under whose carpet and dust are swept the details. In boldly direct language, Jaime Luis offers us a needed reminder that, in the ultimate position, the side anyone is on is their own. And, even with best intentions, too many innocents are assigned to hell. *Fanon City Meu* will serve as cautionary vignettes we cannot afford to forget.

— **John Landry,** author of *who will prune the plum tree when I'm gone*

I was stunned and mesmerized by *Fanon City Meu*. Jaime Huenún's words assail us with the raw realities of our world, reminding us that committed poetry makes the connections, between struggles, between worlds, between hearts. Piling image upon image, in a way that invokes the most daring of Neruda's poems, Huenún wades into the roiling storms of our era, crushing cynicism and demanding action.

— **Rick Ayers,** author of *Teaching the Taboo: Courage and Imagination in the Classroom* and *An Empty Seat in Class: Teaching and Learning after the Death of a Student*

Fanon City Meu

Jaime Luis Huenún

Translated from the Spanish by
Thomas Rothe

Introduction by
Urayoán Noel

DIÁLOGOS
BOOKS

Fanon City Meu

Jaime Luis Huenún

Translated by Thomas Rothe

Copyright © 2017 by Das Kapital Ediciones, Jaime Luis Huenún,
Thomas Rothe, and Diálogos Books.

Spanish edition copyright © Das Kapital Ediciones,
Santiago, Chile, reprinted by permission.

Printed in the U.S.A.
First Printing
10 9 8 7 6 5 4 3 2 1   17 18 19 20 21 22

Book design: Bill Lavender
Front cover art: "Junto a Fanon" Acrylic on canson cardboard,
30x42 cm., 2017, by Eduardo Rapiman.

Library of Congress Control Number: 2017947602
Huenún, Jaime Luis
Fanon City Meu / Jaime Luis Huenún;
with Thomas Rothe (translator)
p. cm.
ISBN: 978-1-944884-28-4 (pbk.)

DIÁLOGOS
BOOKS
dialogosbooks.com

Índice

Entonces caímos en Ciudad Fanon   24

Vivir en Ciudad Fanon no era más   26

Allá abajo, en los pliegues   28

Sentí nacer en mí   30

Temblábamos de miedo, te lo juro,   32

Veo la cara de todos en Ciudad Fanon,   34

El amor acabará contigo —me dicen.   36

La lluvia padece de la noche.   38

"Si yo fuera un pardo indio   40

Seguimos el Sendero Luminoso   42

Los ancianos montoneros argentinos   44

La alegría de los héroes   46

En sellada vasija de formol   48

Bandadas de sicarios   50

Nadie más murió conmigo, mis hermanos,   52

Duermo otra vez junto al río que arrastra   54

Fuego en el Bar Alabama,   56

Un castillo en los ojos de Jaime Cruzeiro,   58

La vidente lucumí,   60

Liberamos a Vallejo de la cárcel   62

Canturrear entre las flores no es difícil,   64

Contents

Introduction: Notes on a Geopoetic City   xiv

Translator's Note   xvii

Then we fell into Fanon City   25

Life in Fanon City was reduced   27

Down there in the tattered   29

I felt the blades of a knife   31

We trembled with fear, I swear,   33

I see everyone's face in Fanon City,   35

Love will finish you —they tell me.   37

Rain suffers from the night.   39

"If I were a black Indian   41

We followed Shining Path   43

The veteran Argentine Montoneros   45

The heroes rejoiced   47

We sent Atahualpa's head   49

Flocks of hitmen   51

No one died with me, brothers,   53

Once again I sleep along the river that carries   55

Flames in Bar Alabama,   57

A castle in the eyes of Jaime Cruzeiro,   59

The Lucumi prophet,   61

We broke Vallejo out of jail   63

The challenge is not to hum among flowers,   65

Las manos de Guevara busqué de pueblo en pueblo 66

"Ten cuidado con los cantos nacionales", 68

Sin dinero regresamos a Las Indias 70

El Señor de los Cielos trajo el agua, 72

Encontramos a Rugama en plena puerta 74

No le pidan más dinero a la poesía, 76

La noche: 78

Los pies de Abebe Bikila 80

Mi país es una nave en movimiento. 82

Nuestros dioses son anales, 84

Cual marrano portugués 86

Ahora subes presuroso a la avioneta 88

Constelación del delirio soy, 90

No vivo ya en mi nombre, camaradas, 92

I chased Guevara's hands from town to town   67

"Beware of national anthems,"   69

We returned to The Indies penniless   71

The Lord of the Skies brought water,   73

We found Rugama in the doorway   75

Don't ask poetry for more money,   77

Night: 79

White guards carried   81

My country is a moving ship.   83

Our gods are annals,   85

Like a Portuguese Marrano   *87*

Now you hastily board the small plane   89

I am a constellation of delusions,   91

No longer do I live in my name, comrades,   93

Glossary   96

Introduction: Notes on a Geopoetic City

Like the haunting titular city in his 2001 book *Puerto Trakl* (*Port Trakl*, trans. Daniel Borzutzky, 2008), Huilliche/Mapuche/Chilean poet Jaime Luis Huenún's "Fanon City" is also a geopoetic city. By this I do not mean that it is fictive, although it surely is. Rather I mean that it translates lived and historic and imagined spaces into an unmappable geography. Like the ironic neoliberal arcadia of "Port Trakl," "Fanon City" is also a "contact zone": both cities function as what Mary Louise Pratt famously described as "social spaces where cultures meet, clash, and grapple with each other, often in contexts of highly asymmetrical relations of power, such as colonialism, slavery, or their aftermaths as they are lived out in the world today." But there is no arcadia here, even of the ironic kind. If even the most sophisticated digital map could not contain the human and affective flows that shape "Fanon City," the key here, as in Fanon's work, is an auto-ethnographic struggle rendered precisely in all its ugly beauty, in all its lucid wit and cleansing fury.

The choice of Pernambuco as opening location is significant. The state of Pernambuco, in northeastern Brazil, was both a hub of the African slave trade and an indigenous (Tupi-Guarani) center. By populating his "Fanon City" with those "exiled from Pernambuco" Huenún is placing us at the crux, the matrix of colonialism in the Americas, where the border between the indigenous (of a place) and diasporic (exiled from a place) begins to blur. Huenún's book is then a challenge to the whitewashed poetic histories of Latin America's "lettered cities" (Ángel Rama) with their carefully airbrushed national poets (think of Neruda or

Huidobro or Mistral in Huenún's native Chile). At the same time, Huenún here opens up indigenous Mapuche poetry (historically marginalized and misunderstood in Chile) to a range of diasporic flows, in the process rewriting pious Latin American histories of settler colonialism, from the foundational logics of European/African/indigenous *mestizaje* to the most recent strains of disaster capitalism, against the backdrop of ongoing state repression against the Mapuche people in Chile and Argentina.

Just as striking as the Pernambucan locale is the choice of a classic epigraph from the unjustly forgotten Léon-Gontran Damas's debut *Pigments* (1937), the first great book of Négritude poetry and arguably the movement's second most important book, after Aimé Césaire's *Notebook of a Return to the Native Land*. If Césaire's *Notebook* plumbs the oceanic depths of diaspora, Damas's book documents and deflects empire's frontal blows. The epigraph's invocation of the reader as co-witness of colonialism's ravages ("tell me about disaster") runs through Huenún's lines, refracting the self decolonially in ways Fanon might dig. Like Damas's, these poems are short and blunt yet often sinuous, like the psychic archipelago they map.

Thomas Rothe's translation wisely and skillfully renders the compressed energy of Huenún's lines in a taut vernacular while retaining their imagistic force. Most impressively, Rothe captures the roots and routes of Huenún's syntax-of-skin in an elegant language at once soulful and searing. Of course, the most important word in the book just may be the "Meu" in the title. It has many possible meanings: in Mapudungun (the Mapuche language) "meu" can be used as a shifting preposition that indicates connection, while in Portuguese "meu" means "my" or "mine." What does it mean that "my" city is also a relational one, where colonial and indigenous languages mistranslate each other and the lyric voice that exceeds them? I am grateful to Huenún and Rothe for making us ask these questions, for urging us to join them in the telling of disaster and survival. This is a poetics of resistance both intimate and implicated, a challenge to normative "political poetry" that finds itself through contra/counter-diction: "I am a constellation of delusions."

—Urayoán Noel

Translator's Note

Fanon City Meu, in its original Spanish version, is already a book in translation. Not only do these poems channel Frantz Fanon's ideas on the psychology of colonialism into a dissonant choir of Third World voices, translating political analysis into art, but they also reveal the routes which language can travel over time and space to take on new forms and meanings. Fanon, born on the small Caribbean island of Martinique, to this day a French Overseas Department, grew up surrounded by the national Creole language, which incorporates African syntax and lexicon. Jaime Huenún, born in Valdivia in southern Chile, grew up surrounded by Mapudungun, the language of the Mapuche people. Both authors, born in places scarred by colonial subjugation, are forced to negotiate between two cultures, two languages. Though both write in the colonizer's language (standard French and Spanish), their work reflects on the problem this presents, and the continual search for a language of liberation. The parallels between Fanon and Huenún are unmistakable, but their connection is only made possible by a process of translation: Creole to French to Spanish to Mapudungun to Spanish, and now to English. "To speak a language is to take on a world, a culture," Fanon writes, and Huenún echoes this idea in his poetry, taking on Wallmapu, Chile, and the Americas.

Many people have helped make this book a reality and their acknowledgment is in order. The foundation was set with Huenún for entrusting me with his poems, Bill Lavender for believing in this project, and Camilo Brodsky and Tania Encina of Das Kapital Ediciones, who published the original version of *Fanon City Meu* and greatly facilitated rights issues. I am very grateful to friends and family who read the manuscript and contributed commentary, support, and encouragement, especially Galo Ghigliotto, Carlos Soto Román, Larry Rothe, Karen Borst, and Elena Oliva. Many thanks to Urayoán Noel for his attentive reading and concise, powerful preface. My most sincere gratitude goes to all those who generously offered to write the notes included in this book.

I would also like to thank the editors of the journals in which some of these poems first appeared, occasionally in different versions. "Then we fell into Fanon City," "Life in Fanon City was reduced," "We sent Atahualpa's head," "Rain suffers from the night," and "No longer do I live in my name, comrades" were published in *RED Ink: International Journal of Indigenous Literature, Arts & Humanities*, Spring 2017, Issue 19.1. "We followed Shining Path," "Flames in Bar Alabama," "The Lord of the Skies brought water," "My country is a moving ship," and "I am a constellation of delusions" appeared in *Cape Cod Poetry Review*, No. 4/5. "Down there in the tattered," "We trembled with fear, I swear," "I see everyone's face in Fanon City," "A castle in the eyes of Jaime Cruzeiro," "'Beware of national anthems'," and "Don't ask poetry for more money" appeared in *MAKE Literary Magazine*, Winter 2017, No. 17.

–T.R.

Fanon City Meu

...uneven cobbles, pebbles that roll away under
  one's feet...

  (Black Skin, White Masks)

Désastre
Parlez-moi du desastre
parlez-m'en

  (Léon-Gontran Damas)

Entonces caímos en Ciudad Fanon
como lentos, blanquísimos cuervos
sobre un quemado maizal.
Los cánticos del vudú escuchamos,
la gorda plegaria de los zambos
exiliados de Pernambuco.
"Oui missié, oui missié",
decían los pequeños cargadores mulatos,
y nosotros, al unísono, largamos:
"Mi buen obrero, no mientas nunca,
y nunca robes, nunca, nunca…"

Then we fell into Fanon City
like slow, bleached ravens
over a burnt cornfield.
We heard Voodoo chants,
the heavy pleading of zambos
exiled from Pernambuco.
"Oui missié, oui missié,"
repeated the small mulatto dockhands,
and we, in unison, replied:
"My good worker, never lie,
and never, never steal…"

Vivir en Ciudad Fanon no era más
que vaciarnos de sudor y de memoria.
Era ir los viernes por la noche
a los tambos cuzqueños olvidados
y mercar ahí, sin dios ni ley,
los poderes infinitos de la coca.
Con los chasquis bebíamos cachaza
de favelas sitiadas por la DEA.
Escribíamos después en las murallas:
"your name is puta\$, your name is OKASO".

Life in Fanon City was reduced
to draining our sweat and memory.
It was reduced to Friday nights
in Cuzco's forgotten relay stations
and consuming, amidst lawless souls,
the infinite powers of the coca.
With chasquis we drank cachaça
from favelas besieged by the DEA.
Later we wrote on the walls:
"your name is puta$, your name is DEKLINE."

Allá abajo, en los pliegues
harapientos de su sol,
la ciudad esconde un parque
de longevos tamarindos.
Nuestras indias venden pieles a sus pies,
adornadas con sombreros
y pesados collares de pirita.

Down there in the tattered
creases of its sun,
the city hides a park
with ancient tamarinds.
Our Indian women sell skins at their feet,
adorned with sombreros
and heavy pyrite necklaces.

Sentí nacer en mí
las hojas del cuchillo.

Había viento afuera,
palmeras que bailaban.

Entonces decidí
en ese cuarto infecto,

sacar de mí el error
doliente de la vida.

I felt the blades of a knife
growing in my flesh.

Outside the wind blew
and palm trees danced.

I then decided
in that infected room

to remove the painful
error of my life.

Temblábamos de miedo, te lo juro,
vigilando en los camiones
a esa chusca tropa de fanáticos.
Chacanas tutelares de bronce y de alpaca
colgaban relumbrando de sus cuellos.
Borrosos tatuajes del Chimú
marcaban sus brazos engrillados.
La orden fulminante fue soltarlos en la sierra
y darles por la espalda
sin ni un asco con los AKA.
Murieron, pues así, en nombre del futuro.
Cayeron, pues así, mirando hacia el pasado.

We trembled with fear, I swear,
guarding the trucks
packed with that bizarre horde of fanatics.
Chakana amulets of bronze and alpaca
hung radiant from their necks.
Blurred tattoos of the Chimú people
marked their shackled arms.
The order suddenly came
to release them in the mountains
and shoot them in the back
unmercifully with our AK-47s.
They died like that, in the name of the future.
They fell like that, looking toward the past.

Veo la cara de todos en Ciudad Fanon,
la cara del niño, la cara del pobre,
la cara de seda de esa muchacha
que busca día a día
el dinero y el amor.
Cada rostro va teñido
por la muerte y el deseo;
cada piel oculta sombras que me anuncian
el infierno por venir.

La desgracia de los hombres ya se sabe:
es haber sido unos niños sin recuerdos ni dolor.

I see everyone's face in Fanon City,
the child's face, the beggar's face,
the silk face of that girl
who seeks money and love
day after day.
Each face stained
by death and desire;
each skin hides shadows that predict
the coming hell.

The tragedy of man is a familiar story:
a lost childhood without memories or pain.

El amor acabará contigo —me dicen.
El amor será un puñal en tu espalda —escucho.
El amor es la cárcel del rebelde —repiten.

El amor es la única justicia —les respondo,
contemplando mi cara deslizarse
por la rota ventana de la oscuridad.

Love will finish you —they tell me.
Love will stab you in the back —I hear.
Love is the rebel's prison —they repeat.

Love is the only justice —I respond,
contemplating my face slide
across the broken window of darkness.

La lluvia padece de la noche.
Llora este pueblo en los espejos rotos.
Yo escucho el poema de las ratas
en la nocturna cavidad del sueño.

Rain suffers from the night.
This nation cries in shattered mirrors.
I listen to the poem of rats
in the nocturnal hollow of dreams.

"**Si yo fuera un pardo indio**
al punto me suicidaría" —dijo usted,
mirando de reojo mi rasgado vestido de percal,
mis toscos zapatones campiranos
de yute y osnaburgo.

Yo pensaba en las calles
circulares de Ciudad Fanon,
en los mil fuegos danzantes
que encendía con bastones
en la fiesta de mis sueños.
No hubo modo de hacerle razonar,
no hubo modo de tenderle a usted la mano.
"Para dirigir salvajes —dijo al fin—
sólo hay un método:
unas cuantas patadas en el culo".

"If I were a black Indian
I'd commit suicide right away," you said,
glancing over my ripped calico shirt,
my crude peasant shoes
made of jute and osnaburg.

I was thinking about the circular
streets of Fanon City,
the thousand dancing fires
I lit with torches
in the feast of my dreams.
There was no way to reason with you,
there was no way to lend you a hand.
"To manage savages," you finally said,
"only one method works:
a good kick in the ass."

Seguimos el Sendero Luminoso
convocados por los Apus
de los cerros de Ayacucho.
Nos armamos con los rifles de Guzmán
y huaracas que tejimos
con pulido cuero andino.
En la sierra se unieron a nosotros
tribus Campas, gente quechua
y unos vagos morenos amazónicos
que debían varias cuentas a la ley.
Nos barrieron en El Yuro sin piedad,
y dejaron nuestros cuerpos
al arbitrio de las moscas,
al regalo de los buitres.
Desde entonces caminamos sin destino
por los guetos y las ferias
de los zambos cimarrones.
Y en las noches robamos las monedas
a la sucia y fea fuente
de las viejas utopías.

We followed Shining Path
summoned by the Apus
of the Ayacucho hills.
We packed Guzmán's rifles
and slingshots woven
from polished Andean leather.
In the sierra we were joined by
Campa tribes, Quechua people
and several dark-skinned Amazonian drifters
who had pending debts with the law.
They slaughtered us unmercifully in El Yuro,
and left our bodies
to the discretion of flies,
to the delight of vultures.
Since then we walk aimlessly
through the ghettos and markets
of half-breed maroons.
And by night we steal coins
from the horrid, dirty fountain
of old utopias.

Los ancianos montoneros argentinos
se tomaron el asilo esta mañana.
Piden pan, televisión, visados varios,
la presencia de cónsules y médicos.
"No luchamos para hundirnos en el fango
de un país que nos olvida en cuchitriles.
Aunque solos y exiliados aún podemos
sostener el armamento entre las manos".
Fue Rodolfo el que habló ante la prensa
con un rubio en los dedos, seriamente.
"Compañeros, no perdamos nuestra fe,
aún no somos unos viejos terminales".
Pronto vino el ministro de inmigrantes
para hablar a los ilustres asilados.
"Todo bien —señaló a los reporteros—
el gobierno se hace cargo de estos héroes".
Hubo himnos, medallas, parabienes
y escolares aplaudiendo en la ocasión.
Hubo whisky, canapés, fotografías
y discursos en la ardiente tarde gris.

The veteran Argentine Montoneros
took over the asylum this morning.
They demand bread, TV, various visas,
the presence of consuls and doctors.
"We didn't fight just to sink in the mud
of a country that condemns us to slums.
Our solitude and exile are no excuse
to set aside the armaments of battle."
It was Rodolfo who spoke to the press, sternly,
with a cigarette between his fingers.
"Comrades, don't lose sight of our goals.
We have yet to reach the end of the rope."
Soon the Minister of Immigrants arrived
to speak with the distinguished patients.
"Everything's okay," he told the reporters,
"the government will take care of these heroes."
There were hymns, medals, congratulations,
and school children applauding at the event.
There were whiskies, cocktails, photographs,
and speeches in the scalding gray afternoon.

La alegría de los héroes
se vivía diariamente
en el hostal "Liberación".
Cada tarde ellos charlaban
con el noble pueblo nuevo
que pedía sus consejos.
Y a pesar de la vejez
y las llagas de sus cuerpos
(el honor de la guerrilla,
la mordida inevitable
de la historia),
nos bailaban tibios sones,
apretando en cada giro
los ansiados, duros muslos
de las chicas amerindias.

The heroes rejoiced
on a daily basis
at the "Liberation" hostel.
Each afternoon they talked
with the noble new nation
who sought their advice.
And despite their aged
and wounded bodies
(honors of guerrilla warfare
and history's
inevitable gnawing),
they danced to mild sones,
squeezing at every turn
the anxious, tough thighs
of the Amerindian girls.

En sellada vasija de formol
enviamos la cabeza de Atahualpa
a tu nuevo domicilio.
La robamos al clan de Montecinos
que mercaba en la frontera
las reliquias del imperio.
¡Pobre diablo, loca y triste
sabandija de altiplano!
Un marrano de la selva vale más
que sus viles palabras
y sus pactos.
Ahora es tuya la cabeza del Inca degollado.
Ahora es tuya su mirada,
su vencida y larga cabellera
sin afeites ni cintillos
que delaten su abolengo.
No la vendas a los yanquis
o a los ávidos huaqueros colombianos.
Ese cráneo es más valioso
que la ampolla de morfina
que te inyectas por las noches.
Guárdala de los rateros y las moscas
que hacen nata en la choza donde vives.
Un gobierno carnal en el exilio
crecerá sin fin de esa cabeza.

We sent Atahualpa's head
to your new address
in a sealed jar of formaldehyde.
We stole it from the Montecinos clan
scalping the empire's relics
at the border.
Poor bastard! Crazed and miserable
Altiplano vermin!
A wild swine is worth more
than his vile words
and treaties.
And now you hold the decapitated Inca's head.
Now you hold his gaze,
his defeated long hair
stripped of the headbands and adornments
that distinguish his lineage.
Don't sell it to the Yankees
or ambitious Colombian gravediggers.
That skull is more valuable
than the flask of morphine
you inject each night.
Keep it from the thieves and flies
who coalesce in the shack where you live.
An exiled carnal government
will grow endlessly from that head.

Bandadas de sicarios
rodearon mi edificio.

Bajaron en sus motos
del Cerro de la Cruz.

Miré yo la llovizna,
los autos, los caminos,

las ávidas pupilas
de un pálido gorrión.

Flocks of hitmen
circled my building.

They descended on motorcycles
from Cerro de la Cruz.

I watched the drizzle,
the cars, the roads,

the avid eyes
of a pale sparrow.

Nadie más murió conmigo, mis hermanos,
en la inmunda taberna *Machu Picchu*,
propiedad de unos gordos gamonales
que hacen tratos con la banda de Escobar.

Yo era chasqui, yanacona de Pizarro,
un espía de reserva, un carroñero
que buscaba la droga sustraída
al Palacio de Conquista del marqués.

De tres tiros me tumbaron los conchudos,
justo cuando los turistas japoneses
se largaban borrachos en sus hummer
al dorado y polvoriento amanecer.

No one died with me, brothers,
in that ungodly tavern *Machu Picchu,*
run by pot-bellied landowners
who do business with the Escobar gang.

I was a messenger, an auxiliary to Pizarro,
a reserve spy, a desperate scavenger
looking for the stolen drugs
in the nobleman's Palace of Conquest.

The cowards leveled me in three shots,
right as the Japanese tourists
sped off in their hummers
toward the golden, dust-filled dawn.

Duermo otra vez junto al río que arrastra
el nocturno otoño a la isla "Hermandad".
Tibia es la piedra que rompe el oleaje,
duro el pastizal crecido en la ribera.
Y el dulce viento de los cementerios canta
como un ave de ajenjo en mi corazón.

Once again I sleep along the river that carries
nocturnal autumns to "Brotherhood" island.
A warm rock breaks the swell of waves,
tough grass grows on the shore.
And the sweet cemetery wind sings
like a bird of wormwood in my heart.

Fuego en el Bar Alabama,
fuego en el centro rojo
de Ciudad Fanon.
Ahí la Regenta ponía gladiolos
frente a largos y turbios espejos
traídos de Francia.
Fuego en el Bar Alabama.
En la esquina
un perro alemán nos husmea,
mientras quicios y dinteles caen
a la ardiente patria de los ebrios.
Hemos cantado en el Bar Alabama,
hemos bailado sobre sus tablas
de arce y pino rojo
entre los serios granjeros del sur.
Las mujeres huyen descalzas del incendio
y se agrupan como nubes oscuras
bajo la leve luz de la Osa Mayor.
Fuego en el Bar Alabama.
Las botellas revientan como astros felices
despertando de paso a los viejos patriarcas
que en sus camas, por un rato,
han dejado de morir.

Flames in Bar Alabama,
flames in the red center
of Fanon City.
There, the governor's wife left gladiolas
below tall, grimy mirrors
imported from France.
Flames in Bar Alabama.
In the corner
a German dog sniffs us,
while doorframes and girders fall
on the burning nation of the drunk.
We sang in Bar Alabama,
we stomped on its floor
of maple and red pine
among stern southern farmers.
Women flee the fire barefoot
and gather like dark clouds
under the soft light of Great Bear.
Flames in Bar Alabama.
Bottles burst like elated stars
incidentally waking old patriarchs
who in their beds, for a moment,
have ceased to die.

Un castillo en los ojos de Jaime Cruzeiro,
unos pocos centavos en su mano derecha
y el viento vespertino en su negra calvicie.
Hace ya varios años que vive sin oficio,
sin planes ni cordura, sin amores platónicos.
Camina cada tarde componiendo conciertos
que silba y tararea en la plaza mayor.
Oh, canción de la piedra, balada de la nube,
tonada de la garza que escarba en los jardines.
Un castillo en los ojos de Jaime Cruzeiro
y niñas celestiales jugando en la glorieta.

A castle in the eyes of Jaime Cruzeiro,
a few cents in his right palm
and the evening wind in his black baldness.
He has lived jobless for years now,
no plans or prudence, no platonic love.
He composes concerts on afternoon strolls
whistling and humming in the main square.
Oh, song of stone, ballad of cloud,
tune of the egret digging in gardens.
A castle in the eyes of Jaime Cruzeiro
and celestial daughters playing in the rotunda.

La vidente lucumí,
heredera de las dotes
nigromantes de su abuela,
taconea ya borracha
sobre rotos adoquines
en el viejo malecón.
Aferrada a los turistas
ya no habla de la suerte
ni de males por venir.
Ahora lleva un fiel demonio
sonriendo y bailoteando
en la faz del corazón.

The Lucumi prophet,
heir to her grandmother's
necromancer dowries,
is drunkenly clattering
over broken cobblestones
on the old esplanade.
Clinging to the tourists
she no longer speaks of luck
or imminent misfortune.
She now carries a loyal demon
smiling and dancing
on the surface of her heart.

Liberamos a Vallejo de la cárcel
arrojando las granadas que nos diera
el tozudo comandante Abimael.

Se cayeron las murallas, las torretas,
la blindada oficinita del alcaide,
y el templete franciscano del fortín.

El poeta se quejaba en una silla,
muy cubierto por el polvo de las bombas,
contemplándonos perdido y sin hablar.

"¡Salga ahora, compañero!"—le gritamos,
traspasando la abertura de la celda
y tirándolo de bruces al camión.

"Ya no creo en ustedes —nos repuso—,
no son más que una recua de rufianes,
vil calaña de la banda de Guzmán".

Lo miramos y le dimos en la madre
bajo un sol que rajaba las arenas
justo frente a las huacas de Chan Chan.

We broke Vallejo out of jail
hurling the grenades supplied by
our mulish commander Abimael.

Walls and turrets collapsed
over the warden's bulletproof office
and the prison's Franciscan temple.

The poet was moaning in a chair,
covered in dust from the explosions,
examining us in a voiceless stupor.

"Get out of here, comrade!" we shouted
as we stepped through the cell's opening
and shoved him headfirst into the truck.

"I lost all hope in you," he said,
"You're nothing but a bunch of thugs,
vile lowlifes from the Guzmán gang."

Our eyes met before we beat him
under a sun that scorched the sand
surrounding the huacas of Chan Chan.

Canturrear entre las flores no es difícil,
florecer en triste fango sí lo es.

The challenge is not to hum among flowers,
but to bloom from miserable filth.

Las manos de Guevara busqué de pueblo en pueblo
por orden del Partido, después de la elección.
Oculto entre pandillas, seguí algunas pistas
que me diera un cobrizo traficante de ron.

"En el barrio Lumumba, frente al Puente Cortado,
hallarás una tribu de arahuacos sin ley.
Ellos guardan los restos que dejó la guerrilla
en cuevas y quebradas del Cerro de la Cruz".

Con el bolso a la espalda traspasé los cercados
y entregué mis reglados al anciano sin voz.
Recocían adentro un hediondo mondongo
que sirvieron en platos de aluminio y latón.

"Las manos de Guevara no se venden —dijeron—,
son ofrendas que dimos a la Virgen del Sol".
Un guardián de sombrero mostró los secos miembros
colgados de una efigie dispuesta en un cajón.

Me marché con la luna, drogado hasta los huesos,
contemplando visiones y sombras de terror.
Una tropa al alba arrasó el ranchería
llevándose a la tribu desnuda al socavón.

I chased Guevara's hands from town to town
sent on Party orders right after the elections.
Covert among gangs, I followed several leads
passed on by a bronze-colored rum dealer.

"In barrio Lumumba, facing Puente Cortado,
you'll find a lawless Arawak tribe.
They preserve relics of the guerrilla struggle
in the caves and ravines of Cerro de la Cruz."

With nothing but a satchel, I opened the gate
and handed my gifts to the voiceless old man.
Inside they were cooking a rancid mondongo
served on flimsy aluminum and brass plates.

"Guevara's hands aren't for sale," they said.
"We already offered them to the Virgin of the Sun."
The guardian in a hat uncovered the dried limbs
dangling from an effigy arranged in a wooden crate.

I left with the moon, drugged to the bone,
contemplating visions and shadows of terror.
At dawn a troop ravaged the settlement
and drove the naked tribe into the caverns.

"Ten cuidado con los cantos nacionales",
me dijeron de pronto al oído
los cetrinos guerreros mocovíes.
Disfrazados de inocentes hortelanos
impasibles esperaban en la aduana
el sellado de sus visas.
"Las canciones matan más que los balazos",
susurraron en la mesa
del agente migratorio.
Se perdieron después entre el gentío
que compraba con sobornos y con ruegos
un estrecho camino a la ciudad.

"Beware of national anthems,"
whispered the pallid Mocoví warriors
sitting next to me.
Disguised as innocent farmhands
they waited impassible in customs
for their visa stamps.
"Songs kill more than bullets,"
they muttered
to the immigration officer.
Later they vanished among the crowd
bribing and pleading to purchase
a narrow road to the city.

Sin dinero regresamos a Las Indias
expulsados por la corte y sus secuaces.
Fue Pinzón quien negoció las armas
y llenó de contrabandos la bodega.
"Las fogosas taínas nos esperan,
poco piden por un polvo en sus hamacas.
Hay guerrillas en la Nueva Granada
y Pizarro paga en oro los fusiles".
Sus palabras fueron música en nosotros
hartos ya de mendigar raciones.
Los negocios son negocios y no hay modo
de parar la fea muerte en este mundo.

We returned to The Indies penniless
expelled by the court and its henchmen.
It was Pinzón who negotiated the arms
and stocked the hold with contraband.
"Sultry Taíno women are expecting us;
it takes little to lay them in their hammocks.
There are uprisings in New Granada
and Pizarro pays soldiers in gold."
His words resonated like music within us
exhausted from begging for rations.
Business is business as usual and nothing
can stop the ugly deaths in this world.

El Señor de los Cielos trajo el agua,
la comida de los niños, medicinas.
Su empleado Moctezuma diligente
repartía las cajitas con regalos.
Al final nos entregó cuarenta rifles
con un sello grabado en las culatas.
"Sean justos y disparen en mi nombre
cada vez que mi gente se los pida".
Ahora somos su rebaño predilecto,
una grey que no le falla ni le miente.
Ahora somos una tropa fiera y santa
los guardianes bien templados de su honor.

The Lord of the Skies brought water,
food for the children, and medicine.
His employee, the diligent Moctezuma,
distributed small boxes with presents.
All together he gave us forty rifles
each with an engraving on the stock.
"Be fair and shoot in my name
whenever my people give the order."
Now we are his favorite congregation,
his faithful and trustworthy clan.
Now we are a fierce and holy troop,
the temperate guardians of his honor.

Encontramos a Rugama en plena puerta
del añoso hotel "Renacimiento".
Muy gentil conducía a las parejas
sin mirarlas ni un segundo a los ojos.
"Compañero, —le dijimos— hay escuelas
levantadas por la patria en tu nombre".
Nos echó un vistazo y en silencio
apagó las tres farolas del umbral.

We found Rugama in the doorway
of the aging "Renaissance" motel.
Courtly, he guided the couples
not once looking them in the eyes.
"Comrade," we said. "The nation
has built schools in your name."
He glanced at us and without a word
turned off three lamps over the entrance.

No le pidan más dinero a la poesía,
no más viajes y subsidios, no más luces;
ya la pobre se ha quedado en bancarrota,
ni una papa encontrarán en su alacena.
Déjenla que se vaya por el mundo,
toda coja, toda enclenque, toda seca,
vieja, sola y afirmada en su bastión.
Se acabó la bonanza, proxenetas,
oh, malditos desleales, azulosos
y barbudos palabreros del montón.

Don't ask poetry for more money,
no more trips or subsidies, no more lights;
the poor thing has gone bankrupt,
you won't even find a potato in her pantry.
So let her wander the world,
limping, sickly and withered,
old, abandoned, leaning on her cane.
The bonanza is over, you panderers,
oh, you damned traitors, you bluish
and bearded mediocre babblers.

La noche:
una mujer que da
la espalda.

Night:
a woman who turns
her back.

Los pies de Abebe Bikila
portaban los guardias blancos.

Cubiertos por su bandera,
en vitrina de cristal,
vimos los restos heroicos.

Honores hubo en creole,
en patois y en papiamento
mientras los niños jugaban.

Doce comunas bailaron
al hijo de los pastores
dejando sangre en el polvo.

White guards carried
Abebe Bikila's feet.

Covered by his flag,
in a glass case,
the heroic remains passed us.

Honors were held in Creole,
Patois, and Papiamento
while the children played.

Twelve villages danced
for the son of the shepherds
treading blood in the dust.

Mi país es una nave en movimiento.
Aquí friego de rodillas día y noche
una inmensa cocina inoxidable.
Con manuales de belleza me embellezco.
Bebo agua de Los Alpes, leo en griego.
Soy la india de los sueños de Occidente,
la sirvienta que oculta con sonrisas
la invencible ley de gravedad.

My country is a moving ship.
Here I spend the days bent over scrubbing
an enormous stainless steel kitchen.
I embellish myself with beauty pamphlets.
I drink water from the Alps, I read in Greek.
I am the Indian woman of Western dreams,
the servant whose smile hides
the invincible law of gravity.

Nuestros dioses son anales,
nuestras mujeres, serpientes.
Canta, viajero, canta,
bebe más de nuestro ron.

Our gods are annals,
our women, snakes.
Sing, traveler, sing,
keep drinking our rum.

Cual marrano portugués
entre indias voy y paso.
Llevo al cuello una estrella de seis puntas
que me quema bajo el cielo tropical.

Like a Portuguese Marrano
I blend in among Indian women.
From my neck hangs a six-pointed star
burning my chest under the tropical sky.

Ahora subes presuroso a la avioneta
en el sucio aeropuerto de Frantz Fanon.
Allá lejos la ciudad es inviolable
luz de aceite en el fin de la galaxia.
Se oyen tiros en los cerros aledaños
mientras bebes muy tranquilo antes del vuelo
largos sorbos de tequila "Centurión".

Now you hastily board the small plane
at Frantz Fanon's dirty airport.
From a distance the city appears impenetrable,
an oil lamp at the end of the galaxy.
Gun shots echo from the surrounding hills
as you quietly wait for the plane to depart
nursing a bottle of "Centurión" tequila.

Constelación del delirio soy,
pero tú no me ves,
pero tú no me escuchas.
Va Dios extraviándose
en mi carne y mi lenguaje
Yo cruzo las aduanas y te oigo:
"Este niño será nuestra blasfemia,
la vergüenza será de nuestro nombre".

I am a constellation of delusions,
but you don't see me,
you don't listen.
God loses his way
in my flesh and language.
I go through customs and hear you say:
"This child will be our blasphemy,
shame will be of our name."

No vivo ya en mi nombre, camaradas,
el curso de las aguas ha iniciado
el tiempo de otro vuelo,
el aire de otro cántico.
No lloren, compañeros,
el universo no cree en el amor
y sólo gira, destruye y resucita
en los ojos infelices del lenguaje.
Ya llegará la hora para ustedes
y serán los padres del cañar,
del cuervo y la torcaza.
Y beberán la terca, infame lluvia
en pueblos donde todos bailan
sólo para dar alegría
a secretos animales insomnes.
No vivo ya en mi alma, camaradas,
mi piel no da la luz que la muerte necesita.
Disperso, confundido,
mi canto busca a tientas
la cura de las sombras,
la ley del vaticinio.
Adieu madras, adieu foulards,
adieu, adieu.
Tras los áridos colores del combate,
ved de nuevo, desandando,
el terrible resplandor de nuestra Historia.

No longer do I live in my name, comrades,
the water's course has introduced
the time for another flight,
the air for another hymn.
Don't cry, my friends,
the universe doesn't believe in love
and only spins, destroys, and resuscitates
in the unhappy eyes of language.
Soon your hour will come
and you'll raise the cane fields,
the raven, and the pigeon.
And you'll drink the stubborn, infamous rain
in towns where everyone dances
only to please
secret insomniac animals.
No longer do I live in my soul, comrades,
my skin does not radiate the light death needs.
Dispersed, confused,
my song gropes for
the remedy of shadows,
the law of prediction.
Adieu madras, adieu foulards,
adieu, adieu.
Behind the arid colors of combat,
look once more to retrace
the dreadful radiance of our History.

Glossary

Altiplano: The high plateau of the Andes, largely covering present-day Bolivia and Peru, as well as parts of northern Chile and Argentina.

Chakana: A symmetrical stepped cross with a hole in the center, often associated with Inca spirituality.

Chasqui: Messengers of the Inca Empire who formed an integral part of the communications system. *Chasquis* would run between *tambos*, or relay stations, in order to deliver information over long distances in a short period of time.

Huaca: Pre-Incan religious monument constructed in the form of a pyramid.

Maroon: A term used throughout the Americas to refer to runaway slaves who established their own independent communities. The Jamaican Maroons are well known for their resistance against British colonial rule during the 17th and 18th centuries.

Marrano: Spanish derogatory term for Jewish converts escaping religious persecution.

Meu: In Mapundungun, the language of the Mapuche people, "meu" means "with" or "in," typically placed at the end of sentences.

Mondongo: Soup prepared from tripe and leftovers, popular in Latin America and the Caribbean.

Son: A genre of music that originated in Cuba in the early 20th century which has since then spread to many other parts of Latin America. It draws on the influences of African and Iberian cultures.

Zambo: In the Spanish Colonial caste system, the term *zambo* refers to people of mixed African and Amerindian ancestry.

DIÁLOGOS
BOOKS
dialogosbooks.com

Made in the USA
Monee, IL
07 July 2026

56544771R00062